ENGAGING
YOUR
ANGELS

by

Emmanuel Maiyaki

ENGAGING YOUR ANGELS

Copyright © 2022

Published By:
Emmanuel Maiyaki Media Ministry

Life Changing International Ministry

Tel:
+44 (0) 7483 140 611

Email: maiyaki90@yahoo.com

ISBN 978-905099-88-7

*Designed, printed and bound in UK
by Print Ministry.co.uk*

Table of Contents

—*Preface*—
INTRODUCTION

Has it ever occurred to you that beyond the physical realities we exist in, there are supernatural realities crafted by divinity for humanity to enjoy the fullness of life? How much knowledge do you really have about these supernatural realities?

The bible tells us that the truth we know is what will set us free. And also in a reversed sense; the truth we don't know will keep us in captivity.

Scripture speaking:

"And you shall know the truth, and the truth shall make you free." John 8:32.

The many truths we don't know are the reasons why we suffer many things that we shouldn't be suffering in life.

Supernaturally speaking, do you know that there is a realm called the *"realm of Angels"?* This realm is Divinely made available for our good.

The subject of *"Angels"* is not such that needs a gigantic introduction as many people are aware of the existence of Angels, whether faintly or deeply, but very few people can boast of having Angelic experiences.

The Hebrew word for an *"Angel"* is called *Malakh*, a word that basically means "messenger" or representative. God created many Angels, of course.

As we go on, there is something crucial you need to know about the number "FIVE". Number five symbolizes many things spiritually, amongst which are: JESUS, GRACE, MERCY, POWER and so on. But as regards our subject of focus here, number five symbolizes the ANGEL. The number "FIVE" is the number of the Angelic realm. This simple knowledge is essential because our aim here is to understand how

Angels operate, their assignments in our lives and how to get them to work for us.

There is this story about a tribe in Australia, when a child reaches the age of twelve, for the maturity of the child to be confirmed, his father will take him into the forest and leave him there with wild animals.

There was this case of a man who took his son into the forest, put a blind fold on him and left him there till the next day with wild animals. While the boy was in the forest with the blind fold, all he could hear was diverse voices of animals but couldn't see them since he had a bind fold on him (the rule is to never take off the blind fold). He was so terrified and kept praying to survive it. But there was something he didn't know, it was the fact that his father was actually still there with him in the forest to prevent any harm from coming to him. The father stood there with him in the forest, but he thought he was alone because of the blind fold he had on.

Just like this little boy was terrified at hearing the diverse voices of animals not knowing his father was still watching over him, many people are terrified about living life because of the many negative voices they keep hearing, not knowing that Angels are positioned to watch over them. You may not see the Angels physically, but they are with you.

As you study through this book, you need to take the Angelic truths and knowledge practically and seriously.

Don't just study to have head knowledge, be practical.

The truths in this book will propel you to unimaginable and unexplainable heights of supernatural help and goodness.

Get set for unsurmountable victories and exploits by the supernatural help of Angels.

Chapter One

UNDERSTANDING THE MINISTRY OF ANGELS

The conscious knowledge that so many believers have about demonic activities are seemly more than the knowledge they have about the Ministry of Angels.

Some people can tell you so much about demonic attacks, familiar spirits and sorcery but know nothing about the Angels which God assigned for our good. Angels are given to us to help us, but if we don't use them we can't have victory.

WHO ARE ANGELS?

Angels are ministering spirits sent to help the advancement of the course of your destiny in life.

Scripture speaking:
Are they not all ministering spirits sent forth to minister for those who will inherit salvation? Hebrews 1:14.

Angels are there to minister for you; meaning they are there to take care of your needs at all times. But the big question you need to ask yourself is: how do I relate with Angels and get them to work for me?

Now, after the release of the Holy spirit upon humanity in Acts chapter 2:2-4. Humanity became spiritually empowered to have unblocked access to the realms of the Holy Spirit.

Scripture speaking:
And suddenly there came a sound from heaven, as of a rushing mighty wind, and it filled the whole house where they were sitting.
Then there appeared to them divided tongues, as of fire, and one sat upon each of them.
And they were all filled with the Holy Spirit and began to speak with other tongues, as the Spirit gave them utterance. Acts 2:2-4.

From this point, it is absolutely essential for you to know that the Holy Spirit is the head of all spirits, and just as we saw in scriptures, Angels are "ministering Spirits"; the

Angels are ministering spirits that work alongside with the Holy Spirit to bring about Divine intervention in human endeavors.

Angels have been in existence and in operation right from the beginning. If you check the old testament (Genesis to Malachi) you will see lots of angelic operations which we don't see in our days even with the fact that we are in the dispensation of the Holy Spirit. Why? Because people are not engaging their Angels as a result of so much doubts.

Angels are wired to do different things, every Angel has the specification of his assignment per time in your life.

—Chapter Two—
ANGELS OF FIRE

These Angels are the custodians of fire and chariots of fire. They carry out their operations with fire.

In the bible there is a story about how prophet Elisha kept on exposing the secret plans of the king of Syria and the king thought there was an informant amongst his people. He was then told that there is a prophet in Israel who always exposes his plots of attack on the Israelites. So, the king of Syria prepared an army and came to apprehend Elisha the prophet. (2Kings 6:8-14). Now, when the servant of the prophet (Gehazi) saw the great Army that surrounded them, he was so terrified and cried out.

Scripture speaking:

And when the servant of the man of God arose early and went out, there was an army, surrounding the city with horses and chariots. And his servant said to him, "Alas, my master! What shall we do?" 2Kings 6:15.

Then the prophet Elisha gave him a very amazing answer: *"Do not fear, for those who are with us are more than those who are with them."*

You can tell clearly that Elisha was a man that was conscious of the ministry of Angels and what Angels can do.

Then Elisha prayed for God to open the eyes of his servant, and said, "LORD, I pray, open his eyes that he may see." Then the LORD opened the eyes of the young man, and he saw. And behold, the mountain was full of horses and chariots of fire Angels all around Elisha (2Kings 6:16-17).

Many believers also need to pray for God to open their eyes to see the heavy duty Angels of fire available to help them so that they can stop being terrified by the attacks of the enemies. Spiritual blindness has done us more harm than good.Another operation of the Angels of fire(chariots of fire) was experienced by Elijah when he was done with his assignment on earth (2Kings 2:1-10). He was taken up by the chariots of fire into heaven.

Scripture speaking:

Then it happened, as they continued on and talked, that suddenly a chariot of fire appeared with horses of fire, and separated the two of them; and Elijah went up by a whirlwind into heaven. 2Kings 2:11.

When you need fire to settle any matter in your life, all you need is to call for the Angels of fire and fire shall settle the matter.

—*Chapter Three*—
ANGELS OF WARFARE

There are Angels specifically assigned to handle spiritual warfare.

Angels of warfare are around you to help you fight the battles of your life. Your victory in life can only be taken when you know how to use the forces of the spirit, called Angels of warfare. And this is why the bible says: Not by might nor by power, but by My Spirit,' Says the LORD of hosts. Which spirit? The Angels. The Angels of warfare are your spiritual forces for victory in spiritual warfare.

Scripture speaking:
Then the angel who talked with me answered and said to me, "Do you not know what these are?" And I said, "No, my lord."
So he answered and said to me: "This is the word of the LORD to Zerubbabel: 'Not by might nor by power, but by My Spirit,' Says the LORD of hosts. Zachariah 4:5-6.

With this being said, you need to know how to fight spiritually by engaging your Angels of warfare because the battles of life are first spiritual. So, you need to know how to fight in spirit against opposing spirits in order to get victory in the physical realms of reality.

Scripture speaking:
Finally, my brethren, be strong in the Lord and in the power of His might.
Put on the whole armor of God, that you may be able to stand against the wiles of the devil.
For we do not wrestle against flesh and blood, but against principalities, against powers, against the rulers of the darkness of this age, against spiritual hosts of wickedness in the heavenly places. Ephesians 6:10-12.

You can now see clearly in scripture that there are spiritual principalities, powers, rulers of the darkness of this age, spiritual hosts of wickedness that we wrestle against.

Now, God never deigned you to fight the battles for yourself, which is why

He made Angelic forces available to help you.

Note: spiritual battles in the spiritual realms are only understood by spiritual forces called Angels.

Why does God want you to get Angels involved in your warfare? Let's unravel some mysteries here by looking into Revelations 12:11.

Scripture speaking:
"And they overcame him by the blood of the Lamb and by the word of their testimony, and they did not love their lives to the death. Revelations 12:11.

"THEY" overcame him. Who is the bible referring to here as "THEY"? The bible is not referring to human

beings here. The "THEY" here is referring to the Angelic beings that were working alongside with the Arch Angel Michael in warfare.

From this scriptural analysis, it will be very crucial for you to know that the first warfare that took place on earth did not involve humans, but the battle was fought for the victory and liberation of humans. It was a warfare between the Angels of Michael and the Angels of Lucifer. It was never God's intention for you to fight the devil. But you have been seemingly binding the devil, witches, occultic powers by yourself, that is why nothing is working. You have been binding and loosing for ten years now, yet what is fighting you is refusing to bow, why? because you are not engaging your Angels of warfare.

You can never use unspiritual approach to conquer spiritual battles. It is spirit against spirit.

There are all sorts of warfare in the spirit realm, warfare against sicknesses, poverty, satanic attack, near success syndrome, family barriers, marital crisis, barrenness and so on. Whether you know it or not, most physical tribulations in your life have a spiritual orchestration, your intellect cannot explain this.

Life is controlled from the spirit realm; life in the physical is a byproduct of spiritual creation. The earlier you come to terms with this truth, the better you welcome the ministry of the Angels of warfare.

At a time in Daniel's life, he was troubled because of a vision he saw and the captivity of his people in Babylon was overdue. He was mourning for three full weeks without eating or drinking, as he prayed for their liberation *(see Daniel 10:1-12)*. For about twenty one days, he got no answer because the prince of Persia(spiritual forces) stood against his prayer. Now, Daniel was praying very seriously for these twenty one days, but with his strength and he got no result until the Arch Angel Michael was sent to help Daniel in warfare.

Scripture speaking:
Then he said to me, "Do not fear, Daniel, for from the first day that you set your heart to understand, and to humble yourself before your God, your words were heard; and I have come because of your words.

"But the prince of the kingdom of Persia withstood me twenty-one days; and behold, Michael, one of the chief princes, came to help me, for I had been left alone there with the kings of Persia. Daniel 10:12-13.

So, you can see here in the scripture that the answer to Daniel's prayer was released from the first day he started praying, but some spiritual forces withheld it for twenty one days until an Angel came to help.

The Angel had to do the warfare for Daniel to have victory against the spiritual forces of Persia.

Scripture speaking:
Then he said, "Do you know why I have come to you? And now I must return to fight with the prince of Persia; and when I have gone forth, indeed the prince of Greece will come.
21 "But I will tell you what is noted in the Scripture of Truth. (No one upholds me against these, except Michael your prince. Daniel 10:20-21.

Can you see now that most of the problems in your life, making it look like the heavens are closed over you are caused by the spiritual forces holding back your answers because you have refused to recognize the "Ministry of the Angels of warfare"?

You are undoubtedly going to get formidable results with the ministry of Angels of warfare functional in your life.

The children of Israel were once faced with a warfare which they could not handle on their own, and they employed the ministry Angels of warfare to help them. Just in one night, one Angel killed one hundred and eighty five thousand people which where the enemies of the Israelites.

Scripture speaking:
And it came to pass on a certain night

29

that the angel of the LORD went out, and killed in the camp of the Assyrians one hundred and eighty-five thousand; and when people arose early in the morning, there were the corpses- all dead. 2kings 19:35.

Can you see how powerful an Angel is?

— *Chapter Four* —

ANGELS OF PEACE

The Ministry of the Angels is also tagged with the responsibility of keeping the peace (rest) and seeking mercy for the territories of the world; peace in the nations, society and families etc. This category of Angels are called Angels of peace, they move around to ensure there is peace in the world and plead for mercy on behalf of mankind.

This is also a good reason why Angels should be valued and deployed.

Study *Zachariah1:10-13* carefully and see what the bible says about the Angels of peace and how they gave their report and also pleaded for mercy.

Scripture speaking:
And the man who stood among the myrtle trees answered and said, "These are the ones whom the LORD has sent to walk to and fro throughout the earth."
So they answered the Angel of the LORD, who stood among the myrtle trees, and said, "We have walked to and fro throughout the earth, and behold, all the earth is resting quietly."
Then the Angel of the LORD answered and said, "O LORD of hosts, how long will You not have mercy on

Jerusalem and on the cities of Judah, against which You were angry these seventy years?"
And the LORD answered the angel who talked to me, with good and comforting words.
Zachariah1:10-13.

For instance, there are Angels of peace assigned to your family or nation to keep the peace and seek for mercy, but it is your duty to engage them.

All the persistent chaos and troubles you keep seeing in families and nations are because the many families and nations don't even call for the help of the Angels in troubling times. All the unrest you see around the world today persist because of our inability or unwillingness to recognized the Angelic realms of peace and call for assistance.

This is an uncommon dimension of truth, Angelic ministry carries so much possibilities, and it is high time we consciously and deliberately work with the Angels.

—*Chapter Five*—
ANGELS OF PROSPERITY

But he said to me, 'The LORD, before whom I walk, will send His angel with you and prosper your way; and you shall take a wife for my son from my family and from my father's house. *Genesis 24:40.*

Looking at the above scripture, you will observe that there was an Angel sent specifically to bring about prosperity. This is the Angel of prosperity, the main assignment of this Angel is to cause prosperity to flow in your life.

35

You need to begin by familiarizing yourself with this truth: prosperity has nothing to do with your hard work. I know a lot of people who are working right now but are not prospering.

Working doesn't mean you are going to prosper, salary doesn't make you prosper. Working two jobs or three jobs won't make you prosper.

There are special Angels who carry the supernatural keys that unlock the gates of prosperity, when you have this angelic encounter, you will know that your prosperity has nothing to do with your hard work but has all to do with the assistance of the Angels of prosperity.

These Angels are there to help you because there are things you cannot

do for yourself.
It then means that your prosperity depends on how you use your Angels of prosperity.

WHAT IS PROSPERITY?

Prosperity is not just about material possessions. No, prosperity cuts across the three realms of reality. Prosperity is the supernatural overflow of goodness and abundance both spiritually, mentally and physically in life and destiny.

Scripture speaking:
Beloved, I pray that you may prosper in all things and be in health, just as your soul prospers. 3 John 1:2.

So, you can see now that there is

spiritual prosperity, mental prosperity and physical prosperity. Some people have Physical prosperity (they are very rich, own all manner of landed properties, cars and so on) but they lack mental prosperity (they suffer emotional imbalance, depression, fear, low self-esteem, sorrow, anger and so on).

While some have physical and mental prosperity but lack spiritual prosperity (spiritual prosperity entails prospering in your walk with God and your work for God so as to secure your eternity with God). And vice versa.

With this being said, Angels of prosperity give you all-round prosperity in diversity. Not one sided prosperity, but this still depends on how you deploy them to work for you.

Have you wondered why some people are not prayerful but they are rich? Some did not even go to school but they are wealthy.
Have you noticed that two people will do the same kind of business, one will be succeeding and the other is not? And some people will begin to think that God is partial. No, God is never partial, the only thing is that you did not use your prosperity Angels.

We all have Angelic beings assigned to our lives but not everybody has had experience with their Angels. Many people live and die without having an experience with their Angels. The true success of everybody is tied to the functionality of their prosperity Angels.

Note: Also understand that we have false prosperity. Any prosperity without an authentic root is false. Some people may seem to be prospering visibly but they are perishing from within; they are perishing invisibly.

— Chapter Six —
ANGELS OF PROTECTION

Has it ever happened that some times you are about going somewhere and all of a sudden it looks as if something is stopping you from going? You start your car and it doesn't work and you begin to wonder, why all this?

Many times in cases like this, your Angel of protection is the one preventing you from going out because there is danger ahead.

There are special Angels that God has given charge over you, to keep you secured at all times. They are called the Angels of protection.

Scripture speaking:
For He shall give His angels charge over you, To keep you in all your ways.

In their hands they shall bear you up, Lest you dash your foot against a stone. Psalms 91:11-12.

You need to develop your spiritual life to be sensitive to Angelic interference and assistance because it helps you cooperate with your Angels of protection

Often times when I have some issues in my life, I begin to question my Angels of protection to know why. You must also develop yourself to this level.

Remember the case of Balaam and the donkey.

Scripture speaking:

So Balaam rose in the morning, saddled his donkey, and went with the princes of Moab. Then God's anger was aroused because he went, and the Angel of the LORD took His stand in the way as an adversary against him. And he was riding on his donkey, and his two servants were with him.

Now the donkey saw the Angel of the LORD standing in the way with His drawn sword in His hand, and the donkey turned aside out of the way and went into the field. So Balaam struck the donkey to turn her back onto the road.

Then the Angel of the LORD stood in a

narrow path between the vineyards, with a wall on this side and a wall on that side. And when the donkey saw the Angel of the LORD, she pushed herself against the wall and crushed Balaam's foot against the wall; so he struck her again.

Then the Angel of the LORD went further, and stood in a narrow place where there was no way to turn either to the right hand or to the left. And when the donkey saw the Angel of the LORD, she lay down under Balaam; so Balaam's anger was aroused, and he struck the donkey with his staff.

Then the LORD opened the mouth of the donkey, and she said to Balaam, "What have I done to you, that you have struck me these three times?"

And Balaam said to the donkey,

"Because you have abused me. I wish there were a sword in my hand, for now I would kill you!"

So the donkey said to Balaam, "Am I not your donkey on which you have ridden, ever since I became yours, to this day? Was I ever disposed to do this to you?" And he said, "No."

Then the LORD opened Balaam's eyes, and he saw the Angel of the LORD standing in the way with His drawn sword in His hand; and he bowed his head and fell flat on his face.

And the Angel of the LORD said to him, "Why have you struck your donkey these three times? Behold, I have come out to stand against you, because your way is perverse before Me.

"The donkey saw Me and turned aside from Me these three times. If she had

not turned aside from Me, surely I would also have killed you by now, and let her live."
Number 22:21-33.

You can tell that the donkey had no fault. The donkey was even an agent of preservation to Balaam's life.
In the same manner, many times you attempt doing something or taking some actions but it looks like there is a supernatural being stopping you. Be sensitive, don't force your way and begin to play the blame game like Balaam who was blaming his donkey. Your Angels are on assignment.

Sometimes even in relationships, issues keep arising and it looks like something is speaking to you to end the relationship but you keep on forcing your way in. It is your Angel of protection that is speaking to you in diverse ways, telling you that the relationship won't end well, or that business is going to have a problem, you see all the signs but instead you ignore your Angel and begin to cast and bind rather than follow the Angelic direction you are receiving.

Scripture speaking:
And the Angel of God, who went before the camp of Israel, moved and went behind them; and the pillar of cloud went from before them and stood behind them. Exodus 14:19.

It is your cooperation with your Angel of protection that guarantees the annihilation of destruction and misfortune in your path to destiny. Your spiritual sensitivity needs to be sharp for you to understand Angelic signals. Selah.

—Chapter Seven—

ANGELS OF HEALING

Now there is in Jerusalem by the Sheep Gate a pool, which is called in Hebrew, Bethesda, having five porches. In these lay a great multitude of sick people, blind, lame, paralyzed, waiting for the moving of the water. For an angel went down at a certain time into the pool and stirred up the water; then whoever stepped in first, after the stirring of the water, was made well of whatever disease he had. *John 5:2-4.*

This Angel that went in to stir the pool is the Angel of healing. The Angels of healing are responsible for supernatural healing in all dimensions.

One day, one of my daughters in ministry called me to testify about a healing. Her daughter had cancer of the breast, which the doctor said was three inches in size. She said that after she met me and I prayed for her daughter (a very short prayer of decree), her daughter went back to the doctor and after close examination there was no trace of cancer any more. Now, who do you think removed the cancer?

It is the Angels of healing, they did a

supernatural surgery.

Sometimes some sicknesses and diseases persist in your life because you amplify the sicknesses with your words, you speak too much about the disease and fail to speak the word of God to the Angels of healing.

A nurse that was treating the patients of corona virus was told after being tested by a doctor, that she had been infected with the virus for about nine days. She said, I don't have any virus and I can never have any virus because by His stripes, I am healed.

As God would have it, it was confirmed that there was no virus in her. The Angels of healing heard her decree and accomplished it. Be rooted in the word of God.

Scripture speaking:
But He was wounded for our transgressions, He was bruised for our iniquities; The chastisement for our peace was upon Him, And by His stripes we are healed. Isaiah 53:5.

Do you know that the realm of the miraculous and healing are made possible by Angelic encounter with the Angels of healing?

I once listened to a man of God's ministration and he said, he was trusting God to begin operating in the healing realm. So he kept praying about it and one day, he had an encounter with an Angel of healing. And the Angel began to teach and show him the secrets of the healing realm.

Listen, that health affliction you are currently struggling with will meet it's end once you call for the help of the Angels of healing.
Begin to speak the word of God right now to your Angel of healing.

—Chapter Eight—

ANGELS OF PROVISION

Then as he lay and slept under a broom tree, suddenly an angel touched him, and said to him, "Arise and eat." Then he looked, and there by his head was a cake baked on coals, and a jar of water. So he ate and drank, and lay down again.

And the angel of the LORD came back the second time, and touched him, and said, "Arise and eat, because the journey is too great for you." *1Kings 19:5-7.*

In the above scripture, Elijah was supplied food by the Angel of provision. The Angels of provision handles supernatural supplies. They supply your needs and ensure the termination of lack in your life.

One day I got a call from a lady who has been following my teachings on Angels. She told me that she was so financially down and was owing the council over three thousand pounds. And she said for the first time she placed demand on the Angel of provision based on the teaching she has been hearing.
She placed a demand asking her Angel of provision to send her financial help to clear the debt. She said, from no where the council sent

her a letter, telling her to forget about the debt, that they have a way of covering it up for her. Wow! What a miracle.

Another lady also shared with me how she deployed the Angels of provision to cause financial supply in her life. She said in one day, her bank account got up to six thousand dollars.

You can also get the Angels of provision to supply your needs, if only you will engage them right now.

—*Chapter Nine*—

ANGELS OF DESTINY

Most of the times, we always lay emphasis on the protection of Angels alone, but beyond the protection, Angels are also majorly assigned to take you to your prophetic destiny.

There is a prepared place for you in life by destiny and your Angel of destiny is tagged with the task to keep you on the way and ensure you get to your prophetic destiny. Your Angels of destiny operate supernaturally by divine direction and instruction.

Scripture speaking:
"Behold, I send an Angel before you to keep you in the way and to bring you into the place which I have prepared. Exodus 23:20.

The moment you come to the understanding that the Angel is keeping you and also has the responsibility to take you to where you need to be in life, you will begin to cooperate with your Angel of destiny.

Just like Lot did, he had to cooperate with the Angels of destiny that were assigned to take him and his family to their prophetic destiny and in so doing they were preserved from destruction.

Scripture speaking:
When the morning dawned, the angels urged Lot to hurry, saying, "Arise, take your wife and your two daughters who are here, lest you be consumed in the punishment of the city." Genesis 19:15.

We were going somewhere one day with a friend of mine, and we got stranded because our car could not move. We quickly called some people to come and assist us. As we made attempts to fix the car, we totally ignored and forgot about the fact that there are Angels also assigned to assist us. We ended up being there for about four hours. But listen, Angelic presence brings supernatural intervention into human limitations in whatever case.

In the true sense of it all, if you are not in your prophetic destiny, it then means you are not cooperating with your Angels at all.

WHAT IS PROPHETIC DESTINY?

There is a divinely destined place designed by divinity for the good of humanity in line with fulfilment of purpose and future here on earth.

Your prophetic destiny is a divinely sponsored pattern for the greatness of your life and future in line with what God has said (a prepared place).

Scripture speaking:
For I know the thoughts that I think toward you, says the LORD, thoughts of peace and not of evil, to give you a future and a hope. Jeremiah 29:11.

The guardian Angel of destiny assigned to your life has the responsibility to both protect and lead you. They make sure that you get to your destination in life.
Any time you ignore your Angels of destiny, you are ignoring your safety and direction for destiny.

In order to effectively work with your Angels of destiny to reach your prophetic destiny, you need to develop a supernatural mentality and work with the notion that

Angels are supernatural beings; which means they may be around you actively but you won't see them physically except there is a supernatural permission for you to see them, and this is based on occasional supernatural reasons.

Another major thing to take note of is that, you have to know the assignment the Angel is meant to fulfil in your life. Yes, you cannot possibly work effectively with a person if you don't know the person's assignment in your life, same applies to the Angels. And with this, you can have maximum input from your Angels.

Now, there is a place of your dreams right? There is a place you dream to be in life and it looks like time has been far spent and age is no more on your side? You are already thirty or even forty years old and you are not in the place of your dreams yet because of delays and setbacks?

Angelic presence clears every obstacle and catalyzes speedy arrival at your destined place in life. Don't commonize this knowledge, don't let the enemies pre-occupy you with so much activities but with little results. Learn to employ and deploy your Angels of destiny to work for you.

So, why does it look like we are not getting testimonies in our lives as we should? Why does it look like things delay too much?

Your job, marriage, contract and breakthrough has been delayed just like that and you think all is well?

Many people have left their Angels of destiny dormant, that is why they struggle too much and achieve too little.

Surely, the Angels may be keeping you protected, but you need to get to that place of your breakthrough, joy and open doors and this can only happen when you begin to cooperate with your Angels of destiny by speaking to them.

It should be your prayer duty every day to remind your Angels of all that you desire in life. For instance, you can say: my Angels, you know am not married yet, set me on the path to meet my husband. My Angels, you know I don't have my car yet, make it happen for me. Begin to speak and say: my Angels, in the name of Jesus I activate you, push me, move me even when I don't want to move, I must get there by fire because that is your assignment. I must get to the place of my destiny.

Let us look at it this way, you have been enjoying Angelic protection and security, but what is your reason of being alive if you cannot get to your prophetic destiny?

Note: Angelic presence brings about supernatural movements that set you on the path of improvement in life.

They set the pace of your progression and terminate every retrogression in your destiny.

Your Angel of destiny has all the package to help you, all he is saying is: give me your attention, when I wake you up in the night, wake up. How does your Angel wake you up?

Have you ever slept at night expecting to wake up at a particular time of the night to do something, and suddenly when it gets to that time, you just feel as if someone tapped you to wake up? That is your Angel in action. And also, sometimes you just have a dream that just wakes you up, that is your Angel in action.

There are times when you want to go to bed and sleep is not forth coming, something keeps telling you to pray, that is your Angel of destiny in action.

Don't let your destiny suffer delays any more, deploy the Angels of destiny to move on your behalf.

—Chapter Ten—
ANGELIC ENCOUNTERS

One day, I was speaking with a friend of mine who has been in ministry for over two decades and still counting, all of a sudden he said something very profound, he said: Sir, I just discovered that all the problems we are facing in life is not because of the devil, it is because we lack knowledge. For a while I thought about this and discovered that there was truth in his statement.

There is so much about Angels that we don't know or we trivialize certain relevant knowledge about the Angels and their operations.

The devil is not afraid of you going to church, all he is afraid of is that you should not get more understanding. The devil has no problem with you praying, he wants to give you prayer points that have nothing to do with God.
Be aware, it is not every prayer that you pray that is answered, the kind of prayers that guarantee answers are prayers tied to the will of God.

Scripture speaking:
Likewise the Spirit also helps in our weaknesses. For we do not know what we should pray for as we ought, but the Spirit Himself makes intercession for

us with groanings which cannot be uttered.

Now He who searches the hearts knows what the mind of the Spirit is, because He makes intercession for the saints according to the will of God. Romans 8:26-27.

God never promised to answer every prayer, he only promised to answer the prayers that are tied to His will. This is why the bible says; the Spirit makes intercession for us according to the will of God. You see, there are many prayers we pray that have nothing to do with the will of God.

The effectiveness of your answer prayer is bound to your connection with the will of God. Multitudes of words and babbling in prayer does not move God to answer you.

Let the eyes of your understanding be opened so that you can see what God is doing around you. The eyes of your understanding here is talking about your spiritual understanding for the perception and reception of the invisible realms of Godly realities.

Scripture speaking:
The eyes of your understanding being enlightened; that you may know what is the hope of His calling, what are the riches of the glory of His inheritance in the saints. Ephesians 1:18.

Do you know the reason why fear

exist?

It is because we can't see the invisible realm. We can only see the physical. The fact that you do not see what is happening in the invisible realm doesn't mean it is dormant, in fact the invisible realm has more activities than the physical realm.

Life is controlled from the invisible realm, Divinity operates from the invisible realms which is the realm of faith and the supernatural.
The Angels operate from the invisible realm. Therefore, you connect to the operations of Angels in the invisible realm through the supernatural by faith.
Keep this in mind: the more you

grow in faith, the deeper you are bound to enjoy Angelic possibilities.

A friend of mine shared an experience with me, he told me that when he listened to my message about the Angels, he said he wanted to prove it to know how real it is. So, later that night, he prayed for a period of time and then he said: Oh Lord, I decree and deploy my Angel to wake me up at 12:30 this afternoon. This was his own way of wanting to prove the reality of the Angels, yours could be a different approach.

He said, immediately it was 12:28, something woke him up. He was amazed and his faith was boosted beyond normal. In the same manner, you can take your own step of faith to prove this knowledge about Angels.

Your encounter with Angels is a key factor if you must enjoy Angelic assistance.

Let's look into the life of Moses briefly. After Moses escaped from Egypt for about forty years.

Scripture speaking:
When Pharaoh heard of this matter, he sought to kill Moses. But Moses fled from the face of Pharaoh and dwelt in the land of Midian; and he sat down by a well. Exodus 2:15.

It took an Angelic encounter for Moses to connect with the supernatural realities of God for him to move into his assignment and ministry.

For God to use him, God had to give him an Angelic encounter that caused a drastic and dimensional shift in his personality and spirituality.

Scripture speaking:
And the Angel of the LORD appeared to him in a flame of fire from the midst of a bush. So he looked, and behold, the bush was burning with fire, but the bush was not consumed. Exodus 3:2.

Many people want to prosper in their assignment and ministry but don't want to go to the place of encounter.

Your encounter with Divinity is what confirms your ministry. My earnest counsel for you is: make sure you have an encounter with Divinity before you advance into doing ministry.

Going to bible school is not enough, go for encounter. Bible school will give you knowledge but won't give you encounter. Your encounter is what proves your ministry and assignment. It proves your walk with God.

Which bible school did Peter attend? He was an ordinary fisher man, but his encounter made the difference. Even Paul had an encounter before going into ministry *(See Acts chapter 9).*

Most of the Voodoo priest and fetish dealers here and there are so confident about themselves because they have proven their walk with satan by satanic encounter. You need to do more as a Christian to also prove your walk with God.

By the power of supernatural Angelic encounter, the same Moses that was afraid and ran from Egypt now went back to confront Pharaoh. Can you imagine that?

Scripture speaking:
So Moses went and returned to Jethro his father-in-law, and said to him,

"Please let me go and return to my brethren who are in Egypt, and see whether they are still alive." And Jethro said to Moses, "Go in peace."

And the LORD said to Moses in Midian, "Go, return to Egypt; for all the men who sought your life are dead." Exodus 4:18-19.

If Moses dared to enter Egypt with emptiness, he would have been victimized. Imagine Moses facing the voodoo priests and the fetish dealers in Egypt without any encounter. He would have been utterly destroyed.

The supernatural and Angelic demonstrations right from the burning bush, was God's way of giving Moses victory in the spirit realm.

Your supernatural Angelic encounter enables you to confront and overcome what fights your life and destiny.

Surely Moses had heavy duty Angels working for him and that was how he performed all the wonders that led to his victory against the Egyptians and all the enemies of the Israelites.

Scripture speaking:
"For My Angel will go before you and bring you in to the Amorites and the Hittites and the Perizzites and the Canaanites and the Hivites and the Jebusites; and I will cut them off. Exodus 23:23.

The question for you here is: in what way have you proven your walk with God as a Christian? Do you have any supernatural encounter that confirms your walk with the Angels? Are you just busy being a casual Christian?

Listen, to operate a casual Christian life is to end as a casualty in life. Grow up and own up.

One encounter is enough to give you generational victory in life and destiny.

It is so perplexing in our world today, how Christians comfortably claim to live a Christian life without a single supernatural encounter with an Angel. Then, what is the proof of your Christianity? Or are you just being merely religious?

You just go out there to work and do your business with emptiness, has it not occurred to you that most of the business people who are not committed to God are committed to some sorts of satanic means of getting results? Some of them have even killed their children just to prosper. Some of them have sacrificed so many things.

I once met a lady back in Florida and she shared with me how she made her money. She said, she went into the group of the illuminati. According to her, the people she saw there were most of the famous people and she was afraid. Then they brought a cup that contained blood for her, and told her to dip her hand and taste the blood.

After she did all they told her to do, she began to prosper in her businesses and endeavors. She received a demonic encounter. At the time I met her, she had three Jets and over four thousand workers. But it wasn't God that gave all these things to her, she entered a satanic covenant by demonic encounter.

You who claim to be a Christian, how will you now prosper without Angelic or Holy Ghost encounter or assistance?

Back in New York (Harlem), I was holding a meeting there and a young man shared a shocking story with us: He said he was so frustrated with life and he wanted to make money. He told me that he usually goes to the grave yard (cemetery) in New York to make a demonic covenant in order to make money. And in the service that night, he put his hand in his pocket and brought out thousands of dollars. I was amazed, so I asked him how he got all that money. He then told me that he made a promise by satanic covenant to use his mother for sacrifice. And his mother was in church that day listening to her son. That is a realm of satanic prosperity which is pure destruction. In the same way, for you as a

Christian to get breakthrough in this contemporary world, you need to have an encounter with Divinity.

WHAT IS ENCOUNTER?

Encounter is the unalloyed access of humanity to the Angelic realms of supernatural movements and operations by virtue of Divine permission activated in the place of desperate and deliberate desire.

There are two kinds of desire here:
1. Desire from UP-DOWN: This is when God by His permissive will, decides to give you an encounter. This was the kind of encounter Moses had. He was only tending flocks at Mount Horeb when God gave him the Angelic encounter of

the burning Bush.

Scripture speaking:
Now Moses was tending the flock of Jethro his father-in-law, the priest of Midian. And he led the flock to the back of the desert, and came to Horeb, the mountain of God.
And the Angel of the LORD appeared to him in a flame of fire from the midst of a bush. So he looked, and behold, the bush was burning with fire, but the bush was not consumed. Exodus 3:1-2.

2. Desire from DOWN-UP: This is when you (mankind) deliberately and desperately hunger and pray for an encounter with Divinity. Paul had this kind of desire when he prayed;

oh Lord, that I may know you and the power of your resurrection.

Scripture speaking:
That I may know Him and the power of His resurrection, and the fellowship of His sufferings, being conformed to His death. Philippians 3:10.

Desire from up-down and desire from down-up both work hand in hand in the sense that, your desire for encounter can provoke the will of God to give you an encounter and vice-versa.

No one ever remains the same after a supernatural Angelic encounter.

The realm of the spirit is real, only those who dare it will excel in faith.

I have come across Christians who don't believe in the supernatural, some say they only believe in preaching the word of God. But preaching alone is not enough and that was why Paul said: *My speech and my preaching were not with persuasive words of human wisdom, but in demonstration of the Spirit and of power. 1 Corinthians 2:4.*

If there is no power in your message, how will people take you seriously? Christianity without power is frustration, and power is a product of supernatural encounter with God and the Angelic realms of reality.

You need to desire and hunger for supernatural encounter so you can live above terrestrial and territorial limitation and oppression.

To take life ordinarily is to end as an ordinary prey to the issues of life.

You really have to desire the move of Angels in your life.

Child of God, you need to stop operating the Christianity of lips-service, go for real supernatural and Angelic encounter in order to enter a better chapter of your life and destiny. Don't just sit there and claim you have so much knowledge about Angels, the question is: what have you done with the knowledge?

What encounter have you gotten by virtue of the knowledge you have?

You need to also understand that Angels have their symbols and colours. Some times you may have encounter with Angels and may not know because you don't understand Angelic symbols.

When you begin to operate in the ministry of Angels, you may not start by seeing them physically, you may feel presence around you or some sort of symbolic supernatural colours.

Some of you that have been waiting to see Angels physically may wait too long, Angels carry heavy Divine atmosphere, so you may just faint if you see one without being prepared, that is why Angels begin to reveal themselves to you first through their symbols and presence.

Take this knowledge with seriousness and begin to desire and hunger for encounter.

Stop sitting quietly in assumption, a quiet mouth is a quiet destiny, nothing will work. Pray and trust God for a supernatural Angelic encounter.

—Chapter Eleven—
HOW TO INCREASE ANGELIC ACTIVITIES IN YOUR LIFE

Get to understand that the more the Angelic activities you see in your life, the happier you are bound to be, this is because Angelic activities help you move beyond the limitations of your personal ability and enhance your capacity to get more results in your life.

One day, I had a dream (vision). In that dream, I saw my Angel, looking so beautiful and glorious. In the dream something fell off my hands, so

I stretched my hand to pick it up, but my Angel told me to stop. And the Angel picked it up for me, then said to me: I have been trying to serve you all my life. Wow! When I woke up, I started asking God the meaning of that dream because I wanted to really understand what God was telling me. And the Spirit of God said, I want to show you what your Angel can do for you if only you can allow him do it.

There are many things that would have been more productive and successful in your life if you actually allowed your Angels do them for you.
The more the Angelic activities you have in your life the more the

assurance and confidence you will have to live a result-full life.

Many things are so hard for you and hard on you because you are doing it on your own. Learn to relax and let your Angels take over.

Be well aware that there is a sure possibility to increase the activities of Angels in your life. The more the Angelic activities in your life, the more easy life becomes for you.

Scripture speaking:
Bless the LORD, you His angels, Who excel in strength, who do His word, Heeding the voice of His word. Psalms 103:20.
Amazingly, most of the things you

pray and tell God to do for you are supposed to be things you should do for yourself, especially in dealing with the Angels. For instance, many people pray that God should send His Angels, God should move His Angels on their behalf. If you pray in this manner, you put back the responsibility on God, which shouldn't be. If indeed these Angels are truly assigned to you, then you should speak to them directly and that is how it works.

Picture yourself having a body guard and each time you need something to be done for you by your body guard, you go and ask someone else (may be your father or friend) to help you command or speak to your body guard. No, this is not how it should be. This is exactly what you do, anytime you pray that God should help you command or send the Angels which he has given charge over you.

You are the one that needs to decide the number of the Angelic activities you desire to see in your life daily. This also means that God has given you the supernatural right to communicate with your Angels and get them to work even without asking Him (God) to help you command them.

The busier the Angels are for your life, the better for your life. Give your Angels the room to get more busy for you, you work too much, let your Angels take over.

In extension, it is also very essential for you to know that you can also increase the speed of your Angels or even slow them down as they get active for you.

Your Angels have the ability to bring you instant breakthroughs and miracles. In fact, the things you spend days and weeks doing can be done by your Angels in a blink of an eye, this is because human activities are natural(physical) but Angelic activities are supernatural. Angels operate beyond the physical realms of reality and this is why you can never explain or understand their speed of operation.

Angels operate and answer to you based on the urgency of your situation and how you communicate to them. For instance, two people called for an ambulance. One is a pregnant woman who is in labour and her water even broke already, while the other is someone who just hurt his leg and needs treatment. Whose situation do you think is more urgent and needs attention? Surely, it will be the pregnant woman they will attend to faster.

In the same way, your speed of Angelic activities are based on the urgency of your situation and what you say to them. There are things that God can do for you through the instrumentality of Angelic forces, but you need to give Him enough evidence in order to command providence.

Note: Nothing commands a strong response like a strong evidence. What you say determines what you see.

Many times, things don't change because you don't have enough evidence for what you are asking from God. Yes, even sometimes you cry to God and nothing still happens because crying is not an evidence. Evidence here talks about your intentions and reasons for asking God to do that which you desire.

Scripture speaking:
But I would speak to the Almighty, and I desire to reason with God. Job 13:3.

God works with your reason (evidence), and in the same way the Angels answer to you based on your reason. It is the evidence you can give to God pertaining your need of the Angels that sponsors Angelic intervention.

Now, let us take time to know what Angels like to do or the pattern of activities they respond to in Psalms 103:20.

Scripture speaking:
Bless the LORD, you His angels, Who excel in strength, who do His word, Heeding the voice of His word. Psalms 103:20.

Angels have strength. Not just that, they excel in strength. Angels are supernaturally powerful, they can move any thing. Not like human strength.

Your faith most times gets empowered when you understand the capacity of the strength of your Angels. They are extraordinarily gigantic and powerful.

Mind you, when we are talking of Angels, please don't confuse the picture to be like those of the little baby angels you see on pictures with small wings (e.g. cupid), no that is not what we are talking about here.

What does it mean to say Angels excel in strength?

This means that Angels have an overwhelming capacity and power to bring about any kind of possibility.

Angelic strength has no limits.

When what you are trying to get accomplished is higher than your human strength, you don't need to struggle to get it done, all you need to do is to deploy Angelic strength to work for you. Imagine having a strong and mighty Angel around you and yet you are allowing the devil to mess around with you? No, that shouldn't be. No one can be against you when God is with you and has given His Angels charge over you.

Scripture speaking:
What then shall we say to these things?
If God is for us, who can be against us?
Romans 8:31.

There is a descriptive record of the capacity of the strength of Angels in the book of Revelations. It was recorded there how Angels held the four corners of the wind with their hands. What an expression of strength! Imagine this kind of strength working on your behalf and getting things done for you.

Scripture speaking:

After these things I saw four angels standing at the four corners of the earth, holding the four winds of the earth, that the wind should not blow on the earth, on the sea, or on any tree. Revelations 7:1.

It was just one Angel that threw down Lucifer to an endless fall.

Scripture speaking:
How you are fallen from heaven, O Lucifer, son of the morning! How you are cut down to the ground, You who weakened the nations! Isaiah 14:12.

All these examples are used here to make known to you Angelic possibilities by their strength, so that you know what to expect from Angelic activities and what to assign your Angels to do for you.

How big is that situation in your life? It can be settled, just bring your genuine reason before God and deploy your Angels to work.

The problem most times is that, you know what the witches, wizards and voodoo priest can do, but you lack knowledge of the capacity of the Angels and that is why you keep being afraid of the false powers. May your understanding open in the name of Jesus!

One day, I was ministering in a meeting in Florida, and God opened the eyes of my personal assistant to see the Angel that stood with me. He said: I saw an Angel beside you, he was so huge that his head was above the church. From that day his value and respect for me took another shape.

At another time I was in a dream (vision), in that dream I was in a supermarket trying to pick up something. As I looked up far from me I saw my Angel standing. Then he lifted up his head from that far distance and was able to see what I was doing. And the Angel said to me: am always with you to see what you are doing, I may not be standing very close to you but at whatever distance I can see what you are doing.

Note: *Angels often times work in accordance to word and the will of God as you saw in Psalms 103:20. Therefore, your submission to the word and the will of God is a major key that will trigger Angelic activities and response in your life. And also, mankind has this tendency to abuse privileges and may be pushed to want to deploy Angels to go on ungodly and carnal assignments and this is another major reason why Angels operate based on the word and will of God for you. Since Angels are holy-spiritual beings, there are things you are not permitted to send them.*

—Chapter Twelve—

ANGELS AND THE POWER OF "AMEN"

Angels say AMEN when your desires are in line with the word and will of God. Your *"Amen"* is the confirmation and agreement with your Angels to bring about your desires.

Scripture speaking:
"And to the angel of the church of the Laodiceans write, "These things says the AMEN, the Faithful and True Witness, the Beginning of the creation of God. Revelations 3:14.

107

See also *Revelations 5:14-Then the four living creatures said, "AMEN!" And the twenty-four elders fell down and worshiped Him who lives forever and ever.*
Study further into Revelations 5:1-14 to see what made them say AMEN.

Amen is not just a church language, it is a language of agreement with your Angels. Keep this in mind and stop saying Amen casually. Some people even deliberately refuse to say AMEN because they feel maybe it is just an ordinary word. And that is where many blessings and Angelic activities are missed.

If you want to cooperate with your Angels, always learn to say AMEN

108

whole heartedly. When you say amen, your Angel also says amen and with this comes the confirmation of your answers.

Now, let us break down what the scripture says in Psalms 103:20 to deepen your understanding: *Bless the LORD, you His angels, Who excel in strength, who do His word, Heeding the voice of His word. Psalms 103:20.*

From where it says:..... *who do His word, Heeding the voice of His word.*

This means that once you know the word of God and know how to speak the word of God, the Angels will move on your behalf. Many times, the issue is that you don't speak the word of God, you speak your problems. Any time you speak your problems, the Angels can do nothing. Angels can only hearken to the voice of His word, what you need is the voice of God's word.

Your word confession and declaration determines Angelic manifestation.

Since the Angels hearken to the voice of the word of God, where can you find the word of God? In the bible is the word of God.

When you speak scriptures, Angels turn it to pictures.

Get the point with clarity: The bible did not say that Angels listen to the voice of God (direct voice), it said they listen to the voice of His word. And God recorded his word in the bible.

This means that you should use your voice to speak His word. When the word of God is projected or spoken with your voice, Angels carry it out because they don't hear your voice, they hear what God said.

When the word of God is spoken, it never returns void, because Angels will carry it out.

Scripture speaking:
So shall My word be that goes forth from My mouth; It shall not return to Me void, But it shall accomplish what I please, And it shall prosper in the thing for which I sent it. Isaiah 55:11.

This means that anytime the word of God is released, God does not come from heaven, there are Angelic beings here who will carry it out.

For instance: Anytime you say, it is written: by the stripes of Jesus, I am healed, God doesn't just come down from heaven to heal you; the Angels will move to accomplish the healing.

This is another reason why you need to have the word of God (the Bible) in you. Spend time to study the bible and declare the word always and your life will experience increase in Angelic activities. Look for a bible portion that addresses your present situations and speak it for your Angels to carry it out. Check your language. Don't paralyze and incapacitate your Angels with your negative words.

What you don't say, you don't activate and what you don't activate, you don't achieve.

Another aspect you need to work on is the area of self-condemnation; calling yourself a sinner and disqualifying your self will further block your Angelic access.

As you make efforts towards godly lifestyle, be convinced that God is pleased with you because He so loves you that He gave His only son for you *(John 3:16)* even while you were yet a sinner.

Scripture speaking:
But God demonstrates His own love toward us, in that while we were still sinners, Christ died for us. Romans 5:8.

God is never mad at you, he wants to help you. Any teaching that keeps amplifying the fact that God is mad at you, is a message from the pit of hell targeted to disconnect you from the help of God and Angelic realities.

Believe that God is pleased with you and He is willing to help you. Look at the story of the prodigal son, how the father welcomed him with celebration despite his errors. He was willing to help his son, he wasn't mad at him. In the same way, God is willing to help you get your life back on track no matter your errors.

Do your best against all ought to speak the word of God to the hearing of your Angels. The accomplishment of your dreams and desires depends on your speaking. Learn to send forth the word.

With this, you should know that the ministry of Angels is not a mere religious talk; Angels are real and ready if you are ready.